THE SALT

by

John N. Merrill
(Footslogger)

Maps and photographs by John N. Merrill

a J.N.M. Publication

1991

a J.N.M. PUBLICATION,

J.N.M. PUBLICATIONS,
WINSTER,
MATLOCK,
DERBYSHIRE.
DE4 2DQ
☎ **Winster (0629) 650454**
FAX **Winster (0629) 650416**

Edited, typeset, designed, paged, marketed and distributed by John N. Merrill.

© Text and routes - J.N. Merrill 1991.

© Maps and photographs - John N. Merrill 1991.

First Published - October 1991

ISBN 0 907496 97 0   ♻ recycled paper

Meticulous research has been undertaken to ensure that this publication is highly accurate at the time of going to press. The publishers, however, cannot be held responsible for alterations, errors or omissions, but they would welcome notification of such for future editions.

Typeset in - Eagle book and bold - bold, italic and plain 10pt and 18pt.

Printed by - John N. Merrill at Milne House, Speedwell Mill, Miller's Green, Wirksworth, Derbyshire. DE4 4BL

Cover sketch - © J.N.M. PUBLICATIONS 1991.

An all British product.

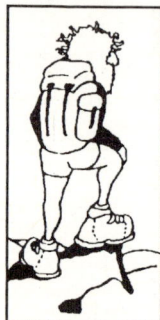

CONTENTS

INTRODUCTION

Cheshire is a county of infinite variety, rich in history, and an adsorbing landscape. The walking is diverse from the plains through attractive villages and past impressive halls to the rugged slopes of the Pennines. Two long distance routes traverse the county south to north - the Sandstone Trail and the Gritstone Trail. The Salter's Way goes west to east. I am indebted to Mr. Michael K.Mooney of Dams Lane, Allostock, who pioneered this route and gave me the opportunity to use his work so that others could follow the way. He is an avid walker and living on a saltway - the way goes past his house - he wanted to learn more about the lane he lived on. From his research the germ of the idea grew to following an old saltway from a major source to the Pennines.

I had walked much of the route before in sections for other guidebooks that I was writing, but the great appeal of this way is tracing an old route. First you walk through the salt fields before following the salt way past Jodrell Bank Radio Telescope. Ahead can be seen the hills! Passing Capesthorne Hall you skirt some of Cheshire's may meres (lakes, which may be natural, the result of flooding of sand quarries, or of subsidence from brine pumping), to cross an old peat moss before the Macclesfield Canal. Rather than road walk through Macclesfield itself the way follows the canal before ascending into the hills from Langley. Here is the sting in the tail to the way, with nearly 18 miles walked you now ascend and descend for the next seven miles to lonely Saltersford Hall, close to the Derbyshire boundary.

I really enjoyed the walk across and saw few people, except in the Tegg's Nose area. You can walk it in a day or spend a more leisurely two days over it. There is accommodation and a campsite close to the route. The only major problem is being collected at the end, because of its remote location. If you can't be met then hike directly to Macclesfield where you can get either a bus or train to where you want to be or back to Northwich. I prefer hiking it west to east as it is more of a challenge - east to west and its all downhill! I hope you have a great walk following the footsteps of the old packhorse teams and let me know how you got on!

Happy walking!

John N. Merrill - Footslogger

ABOUT THE WALK

Whilst every care is taken detailing and describing the walk in this book, it should be borne in mind that the countryside changes by the seasons and the work of man. I have described the walk to the best of my ability, detailing what I have found on the walk in the way of stiles and signs. Obviously with the passage of time stiles become broken or replaced by a ladder stile or even a small gate. Signs too have a habit of being broken or pushed over. All the route follow rights of way and only on rare occasions will you have to overcome obstacles in its path, such as a barbed wire fence or electric fence. On rare occasions rights of way are rerouted and these ammendments are included in the next edition.

The seasons bring occasional problems whilst out walking which should also be borne in mind. In the height of summer paths become overgrown and you will have to fight your way through in a few places. In low lying areas the fields are often full of crops, and although the pathline goes straight across it may be more practical to walk round the field edge to get to the next stile or gate. In summer the ground is generally dry but in autumn and winter, especially because of our climate, the surface can be decidedly wet and slippery; sometimes even gluttonous mud!

These comments are part of countryside walking which help to make your walk more interesting or briefly frustrating. Standing in a farm-yard up to your ankles in mud might not be funny at the time but upon reflection was one of the highlights of the walk!

The mileage for each walk is based on three calculations -

1. pedometer reading.
2. the route map measured on the map.
3. the time I took for the walk.

I believe the figure stated for each walk to be very accurate but we all walk differently and not always in a straight line! The time allowed for each walk is on the generous side and does not include pub stops etc. The figure is based on the fact that on average a person walks 2 1/2 miles an hours but less in hilly terrain.

HOW TO DO IT

Salt has been worked in Cheshire since Roman times. The salt was transported considerable distances from the workings at Northwich, Middlewich and Nantwich to the user. Until the eighteenth century transport was largely by road, the salt being carried on packhorses or in carts. The routes taken by the salters from the Cheshire "wiches" to their customers can be conjectured by the prevalence of place names having "salt" as a component: for example, Saltersford and Salterswall.

This trail of some 25 1/2 miles (42km) follows one of those routes from Northwich to Saltersford, high in the Pennines near the Derbyshire border. In the earlier stages it follows the ancient saltways very closely: in the later stages the route is more conjectural. Very probably the route was through what is now the highly urbanised area of Macclesfield. In order to maintain the pleasure of country walking this trail skirts Macclesfield to reach Saltersford by means of paths and roads through Macclesfield Forest.

Apart from the historical interest of the trail its attraction lies in the wide variety of scenery which it offers, from its beginnings with a back drop of the huge ICI chemical works (based on salt), through the rich dairy farmland of the Cheshire plain to its culmination on the high, windswept and, even today, remote Pennines of Saltersford.

RIGHTS OF WAY

All of the trail is on public roads or rights of way. The latter are, not uncommonly, unlawfully obstructed. If obstructions are discovered the details should be reported to the responsible authority:

Cheshire County Council,
Heritage and Recreation Section,
Commerce House,
Hunter Street,
Chester.

A specimen form which may be used for this purpose may be found at the rear of this pamphlet.

MAPS -

The whole of this trail is on the Ordnance Survey Pathfinder maps - 1:25,000 - Sheet numbers 758 - (SJ67/77) - Northwich & Knutsford and 759 (SJ 87/97) - Macclesfield & Alderley Edge. These maps are almost essential, showing as they do field boundaries and such features as ponds - very useful in establishing your position when the way is not clear on the ground. The Landranger Map - 1:50,000 - Sheet No. 118 - Stoke on Trent & Macclesfield Area - gives a good overall view of the area and ideal for the pickup driver!

HOW TO USE THIS GUIDE -

The trail can be walked end to end in a single day by the fit: those less so may wish to do it in stages. For this reason the guide is arranged in four sections of approximately equal length. The termination of each stage is on a road to facilitate being met by a friend and transported back to the beginning of the stage, to collect the car, or back home, as the case may be.

For those who prefer to walk back to their starting point a glance at the map will indicate many possibilities of circular walks which take in sections of the trail.

For those who complete the way end to end, there is a special four colour embroidered badge, illustrating a salt carrying pack-horse, and a signed certificate available from JNM PUBLICATIONS. They also keep a regisiter of all the people who walk this route.

THE SALT MUSEUM at 162, London Road, Northwich, CW9 8AB; tel. 0606 - 41331 - is well worth visiting to understand more about the value and workings of salt and is situated 1/2 mile south of Northwich town centre.

.... a few grains of salt.

Salt, one of life's major commodities has been extracted from the Cheshire Plains for centuries. At first used mostly for the preservation of meat. In Roman times part of a soldier's pay was in the form of salt. The Latin for salt is *salis* and salt allowance was known as *"salarium"*, from which the word salary originated from. Cheshire's salt area, as today, was centred around the Northwich, Middlewich, and Nantwich. The suffix *"wich"* is derived from the Roman word *Vicus*, which by the Domesday Book, meant a group of dwellings around a brine pit.

Salt in Cheshire is extracted in two ways; by pumping the brine to the surface - hence the numerous brine pumps you will see in the early part of the walk. And by mining the rock salt - this is generally crushed and used on the roads in winter. In Roman times the brine was boiled in lead pans; it wasn't until the 17th century that iron pans were used. The work was very labour intensive. Table salt is made by boiling the brine quickly and when still wet is shovelled into wooden tubs. These form the salt into blocks known as lump salt and were then dried in a hot house. Crystal salt - used for salting fish - was made by slowly simmering the brine. Since the end of last century salt has been made by the vacuum process.

Until the late 18th century salt was transported locally by oxen and cart and overland in packhorse teams. There routes became known as Salter's Way and in Cheshire, as elsewhere, they can be located by the word salt, such as Salter's Lane, Salter's Bridge, and Saltersford. From Northwich a way via Altrincham to Manchester and onto Leeds and York. The route this book follows divided near Saltersford, with one route going via Goyt's Bridge (moved higher up with the building of the reservoir) to Buxton and onto Sheffield or Chesterfield. The other route went to Taxal and over Salter's Knoll to Chapel en le Frith to Stanedge Pole onto Sheffield. The canal took over the transport, with the Trent & Mersey Canal, but this was later superseded by the railways and today it is back on the roads.

Life in the salt works was harsh and often had a devastating effect on the towns and countryside. The uncontrolled pumping of the brine led to land collapsing - today's mere's. Buildings subsided and roads broke up; this led to a bill being passed through Parliament in 1891 known as the Brine Subsidence Compensation Bill. A visit to the Salt Museum in Northwich will tell you more about salt and the dramatic pictures of the subsidence. Today salt is used in just about everything we eat and use.

<u>SUGGESTED FURTHER READING -</u>

"Peakland Roads and Trackways" by A.E.Dodd & E.M.Dood Moorland Publishing. 1980

"British Canals - an illustrated hisory" Charles Hadfield. David & Charles.

Old Broken Cross Inn
beside the Trent & Mersey Canal, Northwich.

Pennys Lane, Northwich to Cross Lanes - 5 3/4 miles (9Km.)

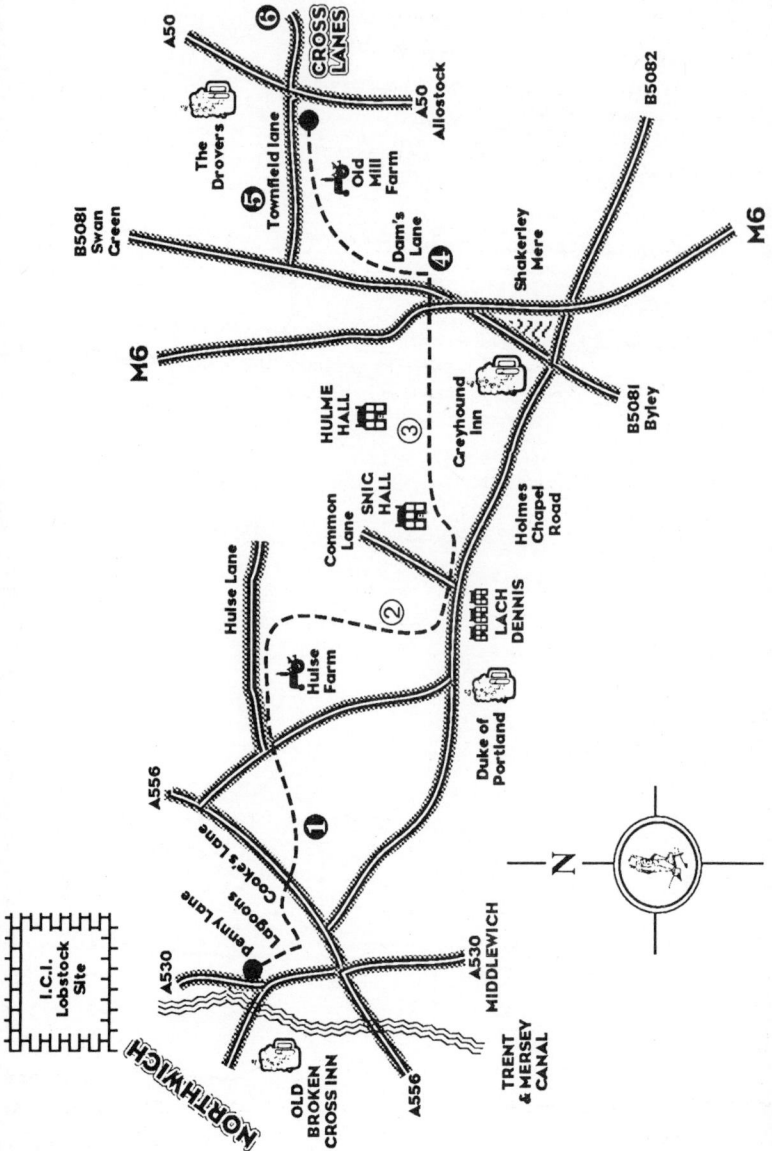

Pennys Lane, Northwich to Cross Lanes.
Approx 5 3/4 miles (9km).

⏹⏴⏹⏴ - Penny's Lane, Broken Cross - Cooke's Lane - Hulse Farm - Lach Dennis - Snig Hall - M6 - Dams Lane - Old Mill Farm - Cross Lanes.

O.S. MAP - 1:25,000 O.S. Pathfinder Series Sheet No. 758 - (SJ67/77) - Northwich & Knutsford.

- Old Broken Cross Inn at start; Duke of Portland Inn, Lach Dennis, just off the route; The Drovers Inn, Cross Lanes, just off the route.

ABOUT THE STAGE - Easy walking along level footpaths and lanes. The trail begins appropriately enough, in the heart of the saltfields and directly in the shadow of one of the chemical works - I.C.I. Lobstock Site - whose basis is salt. A car can be parked in Pennys Lane adjacent to the banks of the ICI lagoons (Grid ref. SJ 685730). Broken Cross is situated 2 miles S.E. of the centre of Northwich beside the A530 road.

WALKING INSTRUCTIONS - Walk along Pennys Lane (this is certainly part of the medieval saltway, the name probably deriving from the penny toll charged) and round into Cooke's Lane. Half way along Cooke's Lane, on the right hand side is a stile and footpath sign. Go over the stile and across the small field to another stile. Cross the A556 (with extreme caution, for this is a very busy road), and go over another stile. Follow the field hedge to its end and then strike out diagonally across the field heading for a single stunted tree. Adjacent to this is a white railed cattle grid: go over it and follow the track, which becomes a metalled access road. The brick structures which you see in the fields around you are the well heads of the brine (salt water workings) which feed the ICI works. Follow the access road until it joins the public road and go directly across, following the sign for Nether Peover.

A few hundred yards along this road turn right onto the footpath just past Hulse Farm - stile and footpath signed "Lach Dennis". Follow the hedge for a few yards and then go directly across the field to a cattle grid. Turn left over the grid along the field hedge to aim for a stile. Having crossed this walk diagonally to another cattle grid in the far right corner. Having gone over this turn left and follow the field hedge to emerge in Lach Dennis to the right of the village post office.

Turn left along the main street for a couple of hundred yards passing Threeways Garage and just after turn left up the public footpath which follows the driveway of Snig Hall. As you follow the path round the rear of Snig Hall and across the fields it is hard to believe that this muddy path was once a main road, and a part of the saltway. About 400 yards along from Snig Hall you will observe to your right a double row of trees about 100 yards long and 30 yards apart: this is a remnant of the old road, the remainder having been ploughed out in the eighteenth and nineteenth centuries.

Continue to follow the field hedges, crossing a drainage channel by a plank bridge until reaching a farm track. The trail turns to the right here but it is worth making a small diversion to the left. A little way along the farm track to the left is Hulme Hall Farm (identified at a distance by the tall cylindrical silo). Although now a mere farmhouse there formerly stood on this site the manor house of the manor of Hulme. The moat and medieval bridge remain. The site is of interest not only because of the moat but because the original settlers here, in the days before the Norman Conquest, were Vikings;"Hulme" is of the same derivation as the common modern Scandinavian "holm", as in Stockholm. The other claim to fame of Hulme is that in the Middle Ages the lords of the manor were the Grosvenors, the family from which springs the present Duke of Westminster, said to be the richest man in England.

Having viewed the site turn back along the farm track and follow it until it becomes a metalled road - Hulme Hall Lane - crossing the M6 motorway. At the crossroads with a minor road - B5081 - turn left and 100 yards later right into Dams Lane. This is a lane of considerable historical interest. Up to the early nineteenth century it was the principal route between Hulme Hall and Over

Peover. It is almost certainly part of the ancient saltway and also formed a means of communication between the Vikings of Hulme and the Anglo-Saxon settlers of Barnshaw (near Goostrey). Halfway along the lane changes from a metalled road to a green lane just after Spinney Cottage and crosses a stream by means of a footbridge. As you walk up the green lane beyond the bridge look to the field to the right and you will see the various humps and mounds which are supposed to be the dams from which the name derives.It is popularly believed that the stream was dammed to work a water mill, hence "Old Mill Farm", adjacent to which the lane joins a metalled road.

Turn right along this road (its name "Townfield Lane" suggests the field left for general use after the majority of the old strip fields had been enclosed) and follow it until it meets the A50 at Cross Lanes. On reaching the A50 you have completed the first stage of the trail. If you have timed your arrival to coincide with licensing hours you may obtain food and drink at The Drovers, a little to the left.

Brine pump
near Hulse Farm.

Cross Lanes to Hackney Platt Bridge - 6 miles (10Km.)

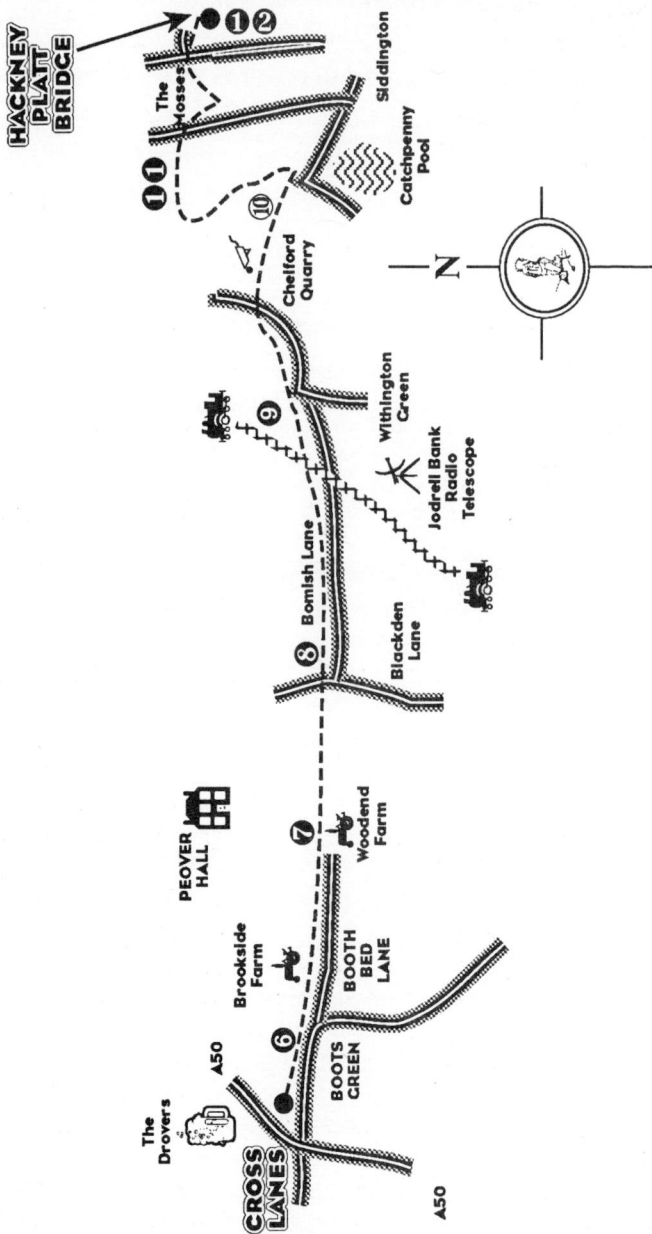

Cross Lanes to Hackney Platt Bridge. Approx 6 miles (10km).

▪▪ ▪▪ ▪▪ ▪▪ **- Cross Lanes - Woodend Farm - Jodrell Bank Telescope Entrance - Daisy House Farm - The Mosses - Hackney Platt Bridge.**

O.S. MAP - *1:25,000 O.S. Pathfinder Series Sheet No. 758 - (SJ67/77) - Northwich & Knutsford. and 759 - (SJ87/97) - Macclesfield and Alderley Edge.*

- The Drover's Arms, Cross Lanes at the start.

ABOUT THE STAGE - Easy walking along lanes and level footpaths.

WALKING INSTRUCTIONS - Cross the A50 and walk down Booth Bed Lane. After a few hundred yards fork left at White Cottage and proceed along the "No Through Road". This soon changes from a metalled road to a green lane which passes through woods. This is again part of the ancient saltway. As you come to the end of this green lane you will see the giant radio telescope of Jodrell Bank, over to your right. When the green lane meets a road turn right and then almost immediately fork left for Withington Green. Follow the lane, still a part of the saltway. Keep left at the next road junction and towards the end of the lane - Bomish Lane - you pass the entrance to Jodrell Bank. If you have the time a visit is well worthwhile to see the telescope at close quarters and to examine the fascinating displays on the universe.

If you decide to save the visit for another day continue until the lane meets a main road - A535 - beside Badger Bank Cottage. Turn left for a hundred yards and then turn into the entrance road to the large sand quarry - Chelford Quarry. Follow the quarry road, looking out for the heavy vehicles, and then, where the road enters a dip, fork left onto a track (just beside the black and white painted barriers of a car park) and, keeping a post and rail fence hard on your right pass through the yards of Dairy House Farm. The sand workings are very extensive and remind you that salt and sand are found in such abundance in Cheshire because much of the County was once under the ocean. Passing though the farm yard notice the many pheasants and the pens in which they are reared. When the farm road meets another road - White Croft Heath Road - turn left and 20 yards later turn left at a stile onto a footpath signposted to Capesthorne.

Follow the path keeping the fence on your right, to cross a track and then a conveyor belt by a footbridge. A few yards further a second bridge crosses a stream. From this strike out diagonally across the field and cross a drainage ditch. Turn right along this ditch and over a stile, along a fenced in path. At a second stile cross into a field and follow the field edge with a wood hard on your right. After a hundred yards climb another stile into the wood: the path then twists and turns through the wood (notice the large number of pheasants) until it reaches an open field. Go across this, keeping the hedge on your left, to emerge onto a road immediately to the right of a small farmhouse.

Turn right down the road - Lapwing Lane - a little way and then left along a bridle track signposted "Capesthorne". Follow this through woods - The Mosses - until meeting a road - Congleton Lane. Cross this and go down Mill Lane to a small brick bridge over a stream: this is Hackney Platt bridge and the end of the second stage of the trail.

Jodrell Bank Radio Telescope.

Old Saltway near Dam's Lane.

Old Salt Way, now a road,
near Jodrell Bank Radio Telescope.

Hackney Platt Bridge to Gurnett.
- 6 1/2 miles (11Km.)

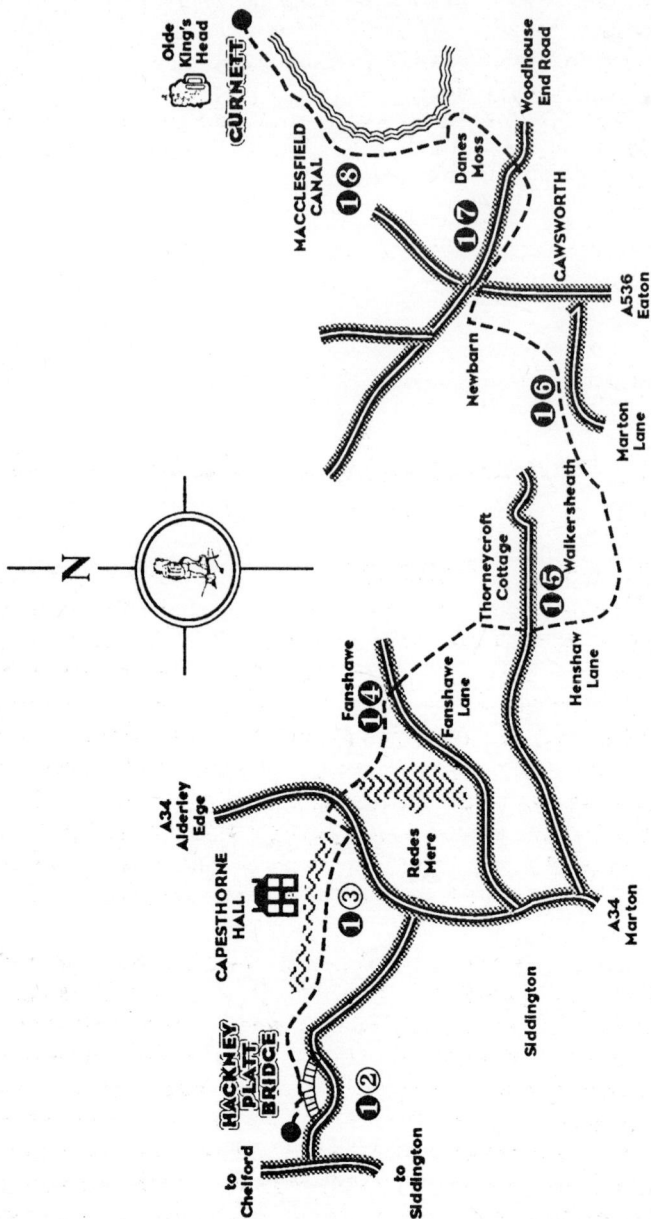

Olde King's Head

GURNETT

MACCLESFIELD CANAL

18

Woodhouse End Road

17

Danes Moss

CAWSWORTH

Newbarn

A536 Eaton

16

Marton Lane

Walkersheath

Thorneycroft Cottage

15

Henshaw Lane

N

Fanshawe

14

Fanshawe Lane

A34 Alderley Edge

CAPESTHORNE HALL

13

Redes Mere

A34 Marton

Siddington

HACKNEY PLATT BRIDGE

12

to Chelford

to Siddington

STAGE 3

Hackney Platt Bridge to Gurnett.
Approx 6 1/2 miles (11km).

`*▀.▄*▄.▄` - Hackney Platt Bridge - Capesthorne Hall Lake - Redes Mere - Fanshawe - Henshaw Lane - Walkersheath Farm - Newbarn - Gawsworth - Danes Moss - Macclesfield Canal - Gurnett.

O.S. MAP - 1:25,000 O.S. Pathfinder Series Sheet No. 759 - (SJ87/97) - Macclesfield and Alderley Edge.

- Olde King's Head, Gurnett.

ABOUT THE STAGE - Easy walking on level paths and canal towpath......the Pennines come into view!!

WALKING INSTRUCTIONS - From Hackney Platt bridge follow Mill Lane, staying on the road for over 1/2 mile passing a couple of houses until reaching a small bungalow on your left. Turn up the track at the side (identified by the signs for "Dinghycraft") and then follow a grassy track just visible as a raised way which skirts the lake of Capesthorne Hall. The house, a large neo-Jacobean structure is clearly visible across the water. On reaching a bridge do not cross (the bridge is private) but instead pass through a kissing gate just to the side and continue around the lake, skirting a wood to come out on a main road; ahead can be seen the outer edge of the Pennines!

Turn left a few steps along the main road and then right along a bridle track which follows the edge of Redes Mere. Pass the gates of the Redes Mere Sailing Club and follow the bridle track as it passes between fences through a wood. When the bridle track joins a gravelled drive turn right. The drive soon becomes a small lane. Follow this to a road, observing as you do so the thatched cottages on your left. Cross the road - Fanshawe Lane - and follow a footpath over a stream. Strike out across the field heading for a stile on the skyline. From here go towards a group of farm buildings, one of them a red painted barn. Clearly visible on the horizon is the unmistakable shape of the telecommunications mast at Croker Hill; to the left is Shutlingsloe and to the right The Cloud. Passing over a stile, walk up a small valley between two fields with a small wood a little to the right. Three more stiles in small fields bring you to a farm road just below the red barn. Turn right down this track to a road beside Thorneycroft Cottage and then cross straight over down Henshaw Lane.

Follow the lane through the farmyard and then, just as you leave the farmyard turn off the track (which descends into woods) and go left through a gate and into a field. Go across the field to another gate with a stile immediately adjacent. Pass into the adjoining field and over to another stile. Cross this and follow the field edge, keeping the fence on you left, to a farm track. Turn right along this and through the yard of Walkersheath Farm to a road - Marton Lane.

Turn left along the road for half a mile or so and then at a group of buildings turn left up a footpath by the side of a small cowshed. Pass through a small gate and head up the field to where a stile and signpost can be seen on the skyline. Continue straight on with the field edge on your right towards a group of farm buildings. Do not go through the farmyard but skirt the buildings (Newbarn) to the left to emerge onto a road - Dark Lane. Turn right down the road to a crossroads with the Macclesfield/Congleton road. Note on the corner the Old Police Cottage with its coat of arms above the door.

Cross the road and walk along Church Lane into Gawsworth village, forking left down Woodhouse Lane. Follow this into Woodhouse End Road until reaching an isolated white painted house called Highfield. Take the footpath at the side the house and follow the field hedge on your left down the long side of the field until reaching a crossing path at a stile. Go straight ahead down a path deeply sunken between trees to a drainage ditch. Carry on along this path following the ditch. You are now on Danes Moss, an ancient peat bog, now a nature reserve. Peat was cut here for centuries: the path on which you are walking is the bed of a horse railway used to haul peat out of the moss. A section of the track can be seen part way along.

At the end of the moss the path crosses a railway line (be sure to check for approaching trains before crossing) and, after a few more yards, brings you to the towpath of the Macclesfield Canal. Turn left along the towpath and follow the canal for 1 1/4 miles to a point where it crosses a road by an aqueduct. Leave the canal at this point by means of the steps down to the road. This is Gurnett, the end of the third stage of the trail. Close at hand is the Olde Kings Head pub where food and drink may be obtained. A little way beyond the aqueduct is Plough House where the famous canal builder, James Brindley, was apprenticed to Abraham Bennett.

Capesthorne Hall.

Redes Mere.

Curnett to Saltersford Hall.
- 7 1/2 miles (12Km.)

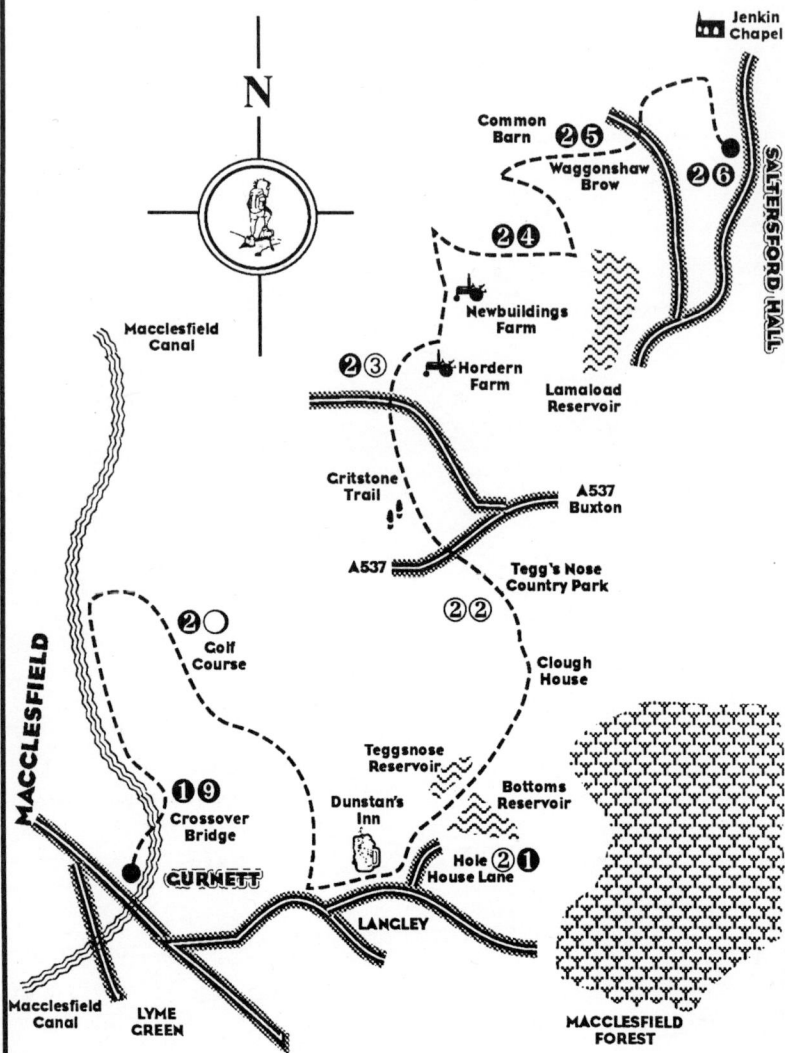

N

Jenkin Chapel

Common Barn **②⑤**

Waggonshaw Brow

②⑥

SALTERSFORD HALL

②④

Macclesfield Canal

Newbuildings Farm

②③ Hordern Farm

Lamaload Reservoir

Critstone Trail

A537 Buxton

A537

Tegg's Nose Country Park

②②

②○ Golf Course

Clough House

MACCLESFIELD

Teggsnose Reservoir

Bottoms Reservoir

❶⑨ Crossover Bridge

Dunstan's Inn

Hole House Lane **②❶**

CURNETT

LANGLEY

Macclesfield Canal

LYME CREEN

MACCLESFIELD FOREST

STAGE

4

**Curnett to Saltersford Hall.
Approx 7 1/2 miles (12km).**

•• •• •• •• - Curnett - Macclesfield Canal - Macclesfield Golf Club - Langley - Teggsnose Reservoir - Clough House Farm - Teggs Nose Car Park - Gritstone Trail - Lamaload Reservoir - Yearns Low Farm - Common Barn Farm - Saltersford Hall.

O.S. MAP - 1:25,000 O.S. Pathfinder Series Sheet No. 759 - (SJ 87/97) - Macclesfield and Alderley Edge.

- Olde King's Head, Curnett; Dunstan's Inn, Langley. Refreshments at Teggs Nose during the season.

ABOUT THE STAGE - The sting in the tail - easy at first then becoming harder as Pennines are climbed.

WALKING INSTRUCTIONS - Continue along the canal towpath. After a little way the towpath changes sides by means of a crossover bridge. At Bridge 40 leave the canal via the steps and turn left up the road. Almost immediately take a right fork and follow the street round to the clubhouse of Macclesfield Golf Club. Walk along the track a few yards, observing the view of Macclesfield which it affords and then go left onto a footpath signposted for Langley. Follow a well defined path as it contours around the hillside. After a little while the path swings to the right downhill towards Langley village. Having crossed a small river by a foot-bridge you emerge onto the main street opposite the works of Rieter Scragg, makers of textile machinery.

On reaching this turn left and walk along this, noting as you do , Langley Hall (now converted into apartments) and a number of three storey cottages. These were cottages occupied by silk weavers who kept their looms on the top floor (the large windows giving the good light necessary) and lived on the ground and first floors. Pass Dunstan's Inn and turn left down Hole House Lane and follow a bridleway between the reservoirs. The bridleway, after a while, comes close to a stream. At a well-defined path to the left cross the stream by stepping stones and proceed up a gated bridleway with a stone wall on the right. Follow this to a small road near Clough House Farm and then turn left up the road for a few yards before turning left up a stone-set path. This is known as The Saddlers Way and is one of the old packhorse routes across the Pennines. At the end of this path you emerge onto the car park of Teggs Nose Country Park. At the Information Centre you may obtain (at least on Sundays) coffee and snacks.

Pass through the car park onto the road and turn right along this for a few yards before veering left along a footpath. This is part of the Gritstone Trail and is clearly waymarked. Follow this path until reaching the Macclesfield/Buxton road. Cross this road bearing leftwards and almost immediately take a footpath (again waymarked as the Gritstone Trail). Follow this past a farm building to cross a stream and strike diagonally up the opposite bank to the junction of two stone walls where there is a stile to be crossed. Follow the way markers to a farm track and turn left, after a few yards leaving the track to climb a stone stile in a wall and then across the fields aiming just to the left of a house in the valley below. Continue down the hill to meet a minor road.

Turn right along this road and follow it for a mile or so to its end at the water works just below Lamaload reservoir. Skirt the works by the footpath just to its right and then follow a path to Yearns Low. Follow the path up the hill passing Yearns Low Farm. The path then becomes a well-defined farm track. A little way on where the track swings to the left leave the track and and head right following a wall. Where this wall meets another is a stone stile. Climb this and make for the barn ahead. Pass through the yard of Common Barn Farm and continue along a marked track. (Be careful not to turn left in the yard along the main farm drive: this is not a right of way and, in any case, will bring you further west than you wish. The proper route is somewhat to the right out of the yard and skirts around Wagonshaw Brow on the left).

At the end of the path you meet a road. Turn left along this for a few yards and then cross a stile on the right following a clearly signed path. Go across the field, being careful not to veer off to the left, to a rather tumbledown wall and, keeping this on your left, head for a long narrow belt of trees. Enter this wood by a stile and go down through the wood to cross a stream by two bridges. Keeping the stream on your right head for a gate giving onto a road. Directly across is Saltersford Hall, now derelict. Note the date stone of 1593.

This is the end of the trail: from here the salters would have continued eastwards into Derbyshire and beyond, perhaps by way of Jenkins Chapel and Pym Chair. While you wait for you lift back to "civilisation" spend a few moments considering the lives of the salters, who made this journey, not once for pleasure, but regularly as a part of earning a living. You may, perhaps, conclude that modern methods have something to recommend them.

View to Tegg's Nose.

Saltersford Hall.

AMENITIES GUIDE LIST -

INNS -

Northwich - Old Broken Cross Inn
Lach Dennis- Duke of Portland
Cross Lanes- The Drovers
Gurnett - Olde King's Head
Langley -Dunstan's Inn

CAMPING -

Northwich - both lie to the west of the town
- Dalefords Manor Caravan Park, The Haven, Dalefords Lane, Sandiway, Northwich. Tel. 0606 - 883391
- Lamb Cottage Caravan and Camping Park, Dalefords Lane, Whitegate, Nr. Northwich. CW8 2BT. Tel. 0606 - 882302

Macclesfield -Jarman Farm, Sutton, Nr. Macclesfield. SK11 0HJ. Tel 02605-2501
Located 1/2 mile S.E. Gurnett at Grid Ref. SK930716.

YOUTH HOSTEL - None on the route, nearest at Buxton - Sherbrook Lodge, Harpur Hill Road, Buxton, Derbyshire. SK17 9NB. Tel. 0298-2287.

BED & BREAKFAST - a random selection -

Northwich -Mayfield Guest House, 200 London Road, Northwich. CW9 8AQ. Tel. 0606 - 43927.

Siddington - Golden Cros Farm, Siddington, Nr. Macclesfield. SK11 9JP. Tel 0260-224358

Marton - Sandpit Farm, Messuage Lane, Marton, Macclesfield. SK11 9HS. Tel. 0260 - 224254

Gawsworth - Roughs Hey Farm, Leek Road, Gawsworth, Macclesfield. SK11 0JQ Tel 0260 - 52286.

Langley -Highlow Farm, Langley, Nr. Macclesfield. SK11 ONE. Tel. 0260-52230.

Macclesfield -Belle Grove, 237 Park Lane, Macclesfield. SK11 5AE. Tel. 0625-613003.
- Park Vale Guest House, 252 Park Lane, Macclesfield. SK11 8AA. Tel. 0625-500025.

TOURIST INFORMATION CENTRE - ℹ️

Macclesfield T.I.C.,
Town Hall,
Market Place,
Macclesfield.
SK10 1HR
Tel. 0625 - 421955 ext. 115/114

WEATHERCALL - N.W. England - 0898-500 416

Olde King's Head, Gurnett.

LOG

DATE STARTED..

DATE COMPLETED...

ROUTE POINT	MILE NO.	ARR.	DEP.	COMMENTS WEATHER
Penny Lane	0			
Hulse Lane	1 1/2			
Lach Dennis	2			
Hulme Hall	3			
Dam's Lane	4			
Townfield Lane	5			
Cross Lanes	6			
Woodend Farm	7			
Bomish Lane	8			
Jodrell Bank	9			
Chelford Quarry	10			
The Mosses	11 1/2			
Hackney Platt Br.	12			
Capesthorne Hall	13			
Fanshawe	14			

LOG

DATE STARTED..

DATE COMPLETED..

ROUTE POINT	MILE NO.	ARR.	DEP.	COMMENTS WEATHER
Henshaw Lane	15			
Marton Lane	16			
Danes Moss	17			
Macclesfield Can.	18			
Gurnett	18 1/2			
Crossover Bridge	19			
Golf Course	20			
Langley	21			
Tegg's Nose	22			
Gritstone Trail	23			
Waggonshaw Brow	25			
Saltersford Hall	26			

Well done - glad you made it!

THE SALTER'S WAY

Badges are white cloth with black lettering and packhorse embroidered in four colours and measure 3 " in diameter.

BADGE ORDER FORM

Date completed ....

Time ....

Name..

Address ....

....

Price .... VAT and signed certificate.

Badges & Certificates are
£3.00 each from -

Happy Walking International Ltd.,
Unit 1, Molyneux Business Park,
Whitworth Road, Darley Dale,
Matlock, Derbyshire. DE4 2HJ
Tel/Fax 01629 - 735911

"I'... Green with white
.... ge and VAT.

From - .... shire. DE4 2DQ
TEL. W... er - 0629 - 650416

.... **You may photocopy this form if needed** ....

THE JOHN MERRILL CHALLENGE WALK BADGE - walk this route twice or complete another of John Merrill's Challenge Walks and send details and cheque for £2.50 for a special circular four colour embroidered badge, to J.N.M. Publications; price includes postage and VAT.

EQUIPMENT NOTES
.... some personal thoughts

BOOTS - *preferably with a full leather upper, of medium weight, with a vibram sole. I always add a foam cushioned insole to help cushion the base of my feet.*

SOCKS - *I generally wear two thick pairs as this helps minimise blisters. The inner pair are of loop stitch variety and approximately 80% wool. The outer are a thick rib pair of approximately 80% wool.*

WATERPROOFS - *for general walking I wear a T shirt or cotton shirt with a cotton wind jacket on top. You generate heat as you walk and I prefer to layer my clothes to avoid getting too hot. Depending on the season will dictate how many layers you wear. In soft rain I just use my wind jacket for I know it quickly dries out. In heavy or consistant rain I slip on a neoprene lined gagoule, and although hot and clammy it does keep me reasonably dry. Only in extreme conditions will I don overtrousers, much preferring to get wet and feel comfortable. I never wear gaiters!*

FOOD - *as I walk I carry bars of chocolate, for they provide instant energy and are light to carry. In winter a flask of hot coffee is welcome. I never carry water and find no hardship from not doing so, but this is a personal matter! From experience I find the more I drink the more I want and sweat. You should always carry some extra food such as Kendal Mint Cake, for emergencies.*

RUCKSACKS - *for day walking I use a climbing rucksack of about 40 litre capacity and although it leaves excess space it does mean that the sac is well padded, with an internal frame and padded shoulder straps. Inside apart from the basics for one day I carry gloves, balaclava, spare pullover and a pair of socks.*

MAP & COMPASS - *when I am walking I always have the relevant map - preferably 1:25,000 scale - open in my hand. This enables me to constantly check that I am walking the right way. In case of bad weather I carry a compass, which once mastered gives you complete confidence in thick cloud or mist.*

THE HIKER'S CODE

❀ *Hike only along marked routes - do not leave the trail.*

❀ *Use stiles to climb fences; close gates.*

❀ *Camp only in designated campsites.*

❀ *Carry a light-weight stove.*

❀ *Leave the trail cleaner than you found it.*

❀ *Leave flowers and plants for others to enjoy.*

❀ *Keep dogs on a leash.*

❀ *Protect and do not disturb wildlife.*

❀ *Use the trail at your own risk.*

❀ *Leave only your thanks and footprints - take nothing but photographs.*

Hi!
- a few notes about Footslogger.

He was born in the flatlands around Luton in Bedfordshire, but his athletic capabilities soon showed themselves on Sports Day and in the football and cricket teams. Although expelled twice from different schools, he moved to Sheffield and was taken out into the Peak District at the age of 6 1/2. Here he ran up and down the rocks and the sense of enjoyment and freedom has never left him. He was hooked on the outdoors for life. By the age of 15 he had 350 books on the Himalayas and other mountain areas and although failed all eight O levels, he was writing a book on the history of mountaineering! At 16 he soloed the 90 foot high school building and the headmaster rushed him off to Outward Bound Mountain School to be properly trained - he thought it was a fantastic holiday!

At 17 he was chosen with eleven others to go on an expedition to Norway, for a month. Since then he has walked more than 150,000 miles in different parts of the world. He has walked The Cleveland Way 8 times; The Peakland Way 14 times; The Limey Way 14 times; The Pennine Way 4 times; Offa's Dyke 3 times; Pembrokeshire Coast Path 3 times; and all the other official paths at least twice.

He is an avid walker and never known to be really tired; likes to carry heavy loads at 18,000 feet and hates having his socks or shirts washed after a six month walk! His ideal day is a 25 mile walk with three bars of chocolate in his pocket. Having worn out nearly fifty pairs of boots he truly lives up to his nickname, Foot-slogger!

OBSTRUCTION OF RIGHT OF WAY

Description of Right of Way
(e,g, "Footpath from Lamaload to Yearns Low")

_____
_____
_____

Nature of Obstruction
(e.g. Locked gate, barbed wire across path etc.,)

_____
_____

Location of Obstruction
(Give Grid Reference if possible.)

_____
_____

Date of discovery of obstruction

_____

Name and address of person making report -

_____
_____
_____
_____

- you may photocopy this form -

Send to -

Cheshire County Council,
Heritage and Recreation Section,
Commerce House,
Hunter Street,
Chester.

OTHER BOOKS by John N. Merrill Published by J.N.M. PUBLICATIONS

CIRCULAR WALK GUIDES -
SHORT CIRCULAR WALKS IN THE PEAK DISTRICT
LONG CIRCULAR WALKS IN THE PEAK DISTRICT
CIRCULAR WALKS IN WESTERN PEAKLAND
SHORT CIRCULAR WALKS IN THE STAFFORDSHIRE MOORLANDS
SHORT CIRCULAR WALKS AROUND THE TOWNS & VILLAGES OF THE PEAK
DISTRICT
SHORT CIRCULAR WALKS AROUND MATLOCK
SHORT CIRCULAR WALKS IN THE DUKERIES
SHORT CIRCULAR WALKS IN SOUTH YORKSHIRE
SHORT CIRCULAR WALKS IN SOUTH DERBYSHIRE
SHORT CIRCULAR WALKS AROUND BUXTON
SHORT CIRCULAR WALKS IN THE HOPE VALLEY
40 SHORT CIRCULAR WALKS IN THE PEAK DISTRICT
CIRCULAR WALKS ON KINDER & BLEAKLOW
SHORT CIRCULAR WALKS IN SOUTH NOTTINGHAMSHIRE
SHIRT CIRCULAR WALKS IN CHESHIRE
SHORT CIRCULAR WALKS IN WEST YORKSHIRE
CIRCULAR WALKS TO PEAK DISTRICT AIRCRAFT WRECKS by J.Mason

CANAL WALKS -
VOL I - DERBYSHIRE & NOTTINGHAMSHIRE
VOL 2 - CHESHIRE & STAFFORDSHIRE
VOL 3 - STAFFORDSHIRE
VOL 4 - THE CHESHIRE RING
VOL 5 - LINCOLNSHIRE & NOTTINGHAMSHIRE
VOL 6 - SOUTH YORKSHIRE
VOL 7 - THE TRENT & MERSEY CANAL

JOHN MERRILL DAY CHALLENGE WALKS -
WHITE PEAK CHALLENGE WALK
DARK PEAK CHALLENGE WALK
PEAK DISTRICT END TO END WALKS
STAFFORDSHIRE MOORLANDS CHALLENGE WALK
THE LITTLE JOHN CHALLENGE WALK
YORKSHIRE DALES CHALLENGE WALK
NORTH YORKSHIRE MOORS CHALLENGE WALK
LAKELAND CHALLENGE WALK
THE RUTLAND WATER CHALLENGE WALK
MALVERN HILLS CHALLENGE WALK
THE SALTER'S WAY

INSTRUCTION & RECORD -
HIKE TO BE FIT.....STROLLING WITH JOHN
THE JOHN MERRILL WALK RECORD BOOK

MULTIPLE DAY WALKS -
THE RIVERS'S WAY
PEAK DISTRICT: HIGH LEVEL ROUTE
PEAK DISTRICT MARATHONS
THE LIMEY WAY
THE PEAKLAND WAY

COAST WALKS & NATIONAL TRAILS -
ISLE OF WIGHT COAST PATH
PEMBROKESHIRE COAST PATH
THE CLEVELAND WAY

PEAK DISTRICT HISTORICAL GUIDES -
A to Z GUIDE OF THE PEAK DISTRICT
DERBYSHIRE INNS - an A to Z guide
HALLS AND CASTLES OF THE PEAK DISTRICT & DERBYSHIRE
TOURING THE PEAK DISTRICT & DERBYSHIRE BY CAR
DERBYSHIRE FOLKLORE
PUNISHMENT IN DERBYSHIRE
CUSTOMS OF THE PEAK DISTRICT & DERBYSHIRE
WINSTER - a souvenir guide
ARKWRIGHT OF CROMFORD
TALES FROM THE MINES by Geoffrey Carr
PEAK DISTRICT PLACE NAMES by Martin Spray

JOHN MERRILL'S MAJOR WALKS -
TURN RIGHT AT LAND'S END
WITH MUSTARD ON MY BACK
TURN RIGHT AT DEATH VALLEY
EMERALD COAST WALK

COLOUR GUIDES -
THE PEAK DISTRICT.........Something to remember her by.

SKETCH BOOKS -
NORTH STAFFORDSHIRE SKETCHBOOK by John Creber
SKETCHES OF THE PEAK DISTRICT

IN PREPARATION -
LONG CIRCULAR WALKS IN STAFFORDSHIRE
SHORT CIRCULAR WALKS IN THE YORKSHIRE DALES
SHORT CIRCULAR WALKS IN THE LAKE DISTRICT
SHORT CIRCULAR WALKS IN NORTH YORKSHIRE MOORS
SNOWDONIA CHALLENGE WALK
CHARNWOOD FOREST CHALLENGE WALK
FOOTPATHS OF THE WORLD - Vol I - NORTH AMERICA
HIKING IN NEW MEXICO - 7 VOLUMES

☞ **Full list from JNM PUBLICATIONS, Winster, Matlock, Derbys.**